WEEK 1. ABANDON YOURSELF WITH CHILDLIKE CONFIDENCE AND TRUST TO GOD, BE AT PEACE.

Despite our sinful nature most people do want to be good, i.e., to follow God's commands and meet His expectations to the best of their abilities -- if only to be simply happy and at peace with their conscience (which only God can provide). On the other hand, "Considering how God treats His friends [in the short run], is it a surprise that He may have so few?" Or, if only not so many "tears were shed over answered prayers." In the final analysis, though, it is our own failings or imperfect faith that are responsible for whatever suffering befalls us.

Yes, God lowered Himself and tasted suffering and death to experience the wretched human condition, to feel what it takes to be man -- and elevate the latter, us, to the status of God's children, forever unconditionally loved, remembered, saved. Lord, you do with me what you want; if only I may beg you to be as gentle and sensible, in my human comprehension, as you possibly wish to condescend. And if I feel abandoned, may music, mystical reading, and Scotch help me out?

But if God expects anything from us in return for His love, is His love unconditional? Unless His expectations only express His wise advice for us to conform with the immutable laws in order to find happiness and fulfillment we so desperately seek. So let's pray for the inspiration how best we can "approach the goal for which God created us."

God's will is fulfilled immediately as His Word becomes, creates, changes, sustains the Universe, gives us life, and lets us feel God's presence if not see His face.

The choice is not always clear-cut: one may die when choosing life or live (in God) by dying for the world. (I wish the latter were simpler and all the temptations and fears easier to eradicate.) But, one may as well live to the fullest and please God in this world, or die in despair -- bodily and spiritually, in utmost abjection from God.

WEEK 2. IT IS I WHO CHOOSE, OR IS IT?

1. Since angels, the creatures infinitely more perfect than humans, sinned, how can we be expected not to…? What's wrong with our free will? Why would one, angel

or not, choose eternal damnation for a moment's glory? Unless that moment is more worth dying for than an eternal life of praising God… Does Satan regret his rebellion? Didn't he achieve his, well, goal of independence or at least a certain autonomy? If he is unhappy, does he try to repent and return to his creator? What does he know that other angels don't? Why all this…?

2. Would man sin without Satan's inspiration? Anyway, pride and self-love being so ingrained in human nature, it takes supernatural gifts rather than a simple act of free will not to sin. And can we really control our thoughts? Nevertheless, we deserve what we receive and should praise God for sparing us, having mercy on us most of the time.

3. Knowledge and wisdom being opposite to innocence, they precipitate rather than prevent sin. How happy must Adam & Eve have been in their state of innocent bliss, without the knowledge of corruption and evil. And even if they were subject to decay and death, would this have affected their happiness if they hadn't realized and feared the unavoidable?

4. I should always be prepared for death. On the other hand, I couldn't possibly function in this world if I were… Fighting the enemy would be much easier if I knew his whereabouts, but since he can masquerade as good and make good look bad, play on my emotions (including charity and pity), etc., it takes a lot of time and experience (sensitive conscience, prayerful attitude) to discern (especially the more insidious) sin. Incidentally, why do I fear death if it can only liberate my soul? Is it because of my sins (fear of hell) or continued carnal desires? At any rate, I do want God to dispose of me as He wills…

5. Please cleanse my corrupt soul, forgive my sins, restore my joy of life, my hope that everything and everybody, including me, make sense or at least you will make sense of us if we fail.

6. Christ wasn't interested in correcting social or political systems. He came to save souls, purge evil from within rather than without (the latter would follow). "If men were decent, the world would be decent."

7. I may have been in hell and of course may return there. But even so, why should I curse God rather than myself for it? My mind does play tricks on me and seems sometimes uncontrollably possessed by Satan, but I can always pray and ask God for help which unfailingly, although not necessarily speedily, comes… Thus, in the final analysis, I'm obviously responsible and should be held accountable for my soul's future.

Gratitude for life, prayer for discernment, strength/faith for action.

1. God doesn't need my intellect to communicate His will (my mind may actually distract me from God); all I have to do is open up and listen with my heart, then act with an alert conscience to really do not what I want but what He wants me to do. To suppress my vainglory, proud ambitions, affectation, self-deceit, etc., and truly offer myself to God, place myself at His disposal, and follow His commands to the best of my abilities. Replace fear with faith and hope, lukewarm conformity with courageous deeds, resentment

and prejudice with love. And above all: never cease to pray for God's grace.

2. I continue my attempts, often unconscious, to impress others, look better than I actually am. Sometimes I'm sickeningly self-conscious, pretentious, insincere… Is it not conditioning, though, to survive and function in this world? How true can I afford to be without destroying my career or family? Also, do my confession and even honest desire to change make me any better? Can I change my human nature? Well, nothing is impossible with God…

3. I am ashamed and repenting of my transgressions, but how much can I control my sinful nature? I wish I could stop the flow of self-centered thoughts, abandon myself to God, love my enemies, do only good, be forever humble and truly Christian. I know I should start now, but I just can't do it on my own, not yet at least.

4. After somewhat depressing soul-searching, hurried confessions, continued preoccupation with office problems, uncertainty about the future of my marriage,

finally comes peace. Gratitude for this evening consolation, the whole day in good health, life in general: I'm still here, corrupt and struggling, but not without hope and faith. Nothing is lost as long as I'm conscious and pray; if only I could love more, but that I am capable of, too, thank God again. Everything will be fine in the long run, God hasn't forgotten me, I am still loved…

5. Please help me suppress my envying, greedy, uncharitable, ambitious ego. It's my weakest spot, open to, and actually inviting, the enemy. The source of perpetual anxiety, base desires, unquenchable thirst for recognition and worldly successes. I am my worst enemy.

6. Neglecting God, a "mindless living" like a spiritual corpse, is certainly a source of desolation. Also the fear of self-deceit and the actual delusions are troubling. Peaceful consolation comes when I finally manage to give up myself to God, and gratefully accept His untiring love. If only I could love so unflinchingly, expecting nothing in return, pure and innocent, ready to sacrifice my own desires or plans.

On the other hand, since we must not love evil, how should we handle true enemies? Oppose their actions and love the persons.

7. Hell is I, it does not exist "objectively," it is a state of soul absolutely separated from God by the soul's very free choice. Every sin and its residue give the soul a taste of hell.

I mean nothing without God, my hope and sense are only in Him.

1. Feeling like a silly fraud, disconcerted and anxious to make up for my half-truths and outright lies… I'm a little man, dreaming my little dreams and gloating over my little successes. What am I doing on this earth? Poisoned thoughts… Yet it's true that billions of souls not much different from mine came and went, leaving almost no trace, forgotten even while sill alive. What good did their suffering do, what sense did they make? Nevertheless, in some mysterious way they had to make sense because they WERE, almost as God IS, their very existence being miraculous in the

cold lifelessness of the material universe, not to mention nothingness.

2. I wonder if I don't delude myself into being more worthless and sinful than I actually am. Exaggerated scruples, oversensitive conscience, hyperactive consciousness. Perfidious Enemy's plot to confuse me, undermine my confidence, get me lost in self-hate and loathing. Maybe, with God's grace, I am not as bad as I think and feel?

3. Obviously, I am no good and mean nothing without God. However, as long as I pray and sincerely desire to follow His commands, do I have to feel guilty about my existence and deeds? I should certainly love to do God's bidding. Can He not just tell me clearly what He wants of me? State exactly what to do every moment? My free will wouldn't be abrogated because I would still have a choice to disobey Him. I just need more clarity and possibly understanding about God's will.

4. Why do I have to bother Mary with intercessions? Incidentally, is it sinful to ask questions with possibly blasphemous implications? If my very being is

originally sinful, could I do much worse on my own? Why wasn't human nature changed with Christ's sacrifice and redemption? Even death seems to continue terrifying us regardless of our virtues and faith.

5. I know I shouldn't fear death any more than birth, or rather conception, yet I am often terrified. Not so much of death itself as of its circumstances, the accompanying fear, suffering, loss of dignity. And then, of course, the absolutely mysterious Unknown. Can we really imagine the unimaginable? If we can't why try?

6. We'll go to what we believe in: Paradise, Hell, or Nothingness. Isn't the latter the worst? Is there absolutely no redemption in Hell, even if Satan should repent?

How attached we become… Purge all attachments.

1. God never deceives us, we do it ourselves. He is gentle and loving, the rashness is Satan's mark. If we feel/sense that something is wrong, it probably is… Do

not compromise to condone any evil because it drowns sinners sooner than they realize.

2. Mood: less alert; mind: less sensitive to life and beauty; soul: sleepy, drowsy.

3. Abandon yourself with gratitude and faith to your Creator - you are because of, and for, Him. Otherwise you'd be lost, helpless, useless. Pray to see and act as you should. Never forget your ultimate destination, imagine this is your last day, month, year, decade. Do, or rather try to do, what you can to be true to God. Consider He may see through your eyes and be with you every moment of the day and night. Be what you want to be, be like God-Man.

4. God is Truth as much as, or rather infinitely more than I am. How absurd is any doubt, how ridiculously thoughtless any contrary speculation. He is hidden only because of the limitations of our mind, the smallness of faith, and the corruption of soul. Do I doubt that I exist? Do I question my desire to love and be loved? Where does it come from, my life and my love? Why can't we remember the obvious?

5. The Last Judgment has occurred -- beyond our time -- and we'll learn its mystery as soon as we die, when we face God, join Him in eternity. In the meantime, how much I regret my godless follies, resentment, envy, pride, selfishness… More so, as I continue my journey to apparent nowhere, I struggle to improve, make sense, love, control temptations, serve only God.

6. Even if I find myself in Hell can I still praise God and blame myself for my fate? Or would I be deprived of any feeling of God's presence and simply unable to pray and love? Lose all hope and joy, and wander in desolation and terror across the barren and abandoned expanses of the spiritual universe?

WEEK 3. LET FAITH, HOPE, AND LOVE REPLACE FEAR. WE ARE NEVER ALONE.

1. Jesus indeed is with me, always watchful and loving, offering His help and advice. I'm never left to my own devices, I can always count on Him. I'm never alone, He is my inspiration, my counselor and advocate; He gives me strength and courage. I must only ask, open

up, listen, and act. Believe that His is the way, and follow it; if I stumble or fall, I'll pick myself up and continue my life's journey. THERE IS SIMPLY NO OTHER WAY.

2. God is more real than we are; we can talk with him by praying. We don't have to imagine Him but only open our eyes (soul's) and see that He IS. Jesus wasn't an earthly king or even a civic leader; he wasn't interested in temporal power or glory, in improving political or social systems, or even in alleviating economic inequities. He detested violence, did not defend Himself by military force, rejected armed insurrections. That's why He died… Why do we "improve" on His message of absolute love and measure God by our rotten standards? "If Christians practiced their faith, the whole world would convert to Christianity."

3. I perceive Christ as a loving, gentle, patient, absolutely trustworthy and wise, infinitely superior and wonderful friend. I want to follow blindly His advice as soon as I hear it. I delight in the peace and happiness He brings about. What more does a man need?

4. Christ is our mediator with God, the first and only human being elevated to God's status. He knows first-hand what we feel, how we suffer and die.

5. Yes, God is with us always, but not necessarily speaking. We cannot, and should not try to, break His silence. He will let us know His will when He sees it fit. We must patiently wait, controlling our anxious expectations and avoiding rash judgments and actions. However, we can always pray, and when we do we are always consoled. God's voice is rarely heard in spectacular visions or raptures, it's more often felt like gentle prodding… God doesn't need to yell or scream, shrill is never His way of expression. His voice brings calm and peace.

6. Christ expects us to do no more than He himself went through, but how inhumanly terrifying His suffering and unearthly His experiences were. How can we dream of truly emulating Him, unless of course God prods and inspires us and gives the required strength and perseverance.

7. Can we count on a call as clear and compelling as that of the Apostles? It seems their faith struck them in a lightning's manner, they abandoned and repudiated their way of life on a moment's notice, they changed their very hearts; or rather God transformed their souls and let them believe and see… Again, without God they would have lived and died in utter obscurity like other fishermen before or after them.

8. Since we have been redeemed once and forever, why do we worry so painfully about everything? Whatever happens, we are saved, aren't we? Following Jesus does not have to involve His suffering and agony, and even if it does we know we won't be alone in it. We're expected to do no more than what we can.

Why the Incarnation? To experience and transform the human condition?

1. Can we really ever grasp the mystery of God's Incarnation? Are our speculations worth anything? Shouldn't we just bow our heads to silently and gratefully acknowledge God's love for us without diluting it by our cloudy reasoning? Christ showed us

how to live and die, do we need to know -- which we can't at any rate -- what God thinks, why, etc.? Jesus didn't question or argue with the Father, but did perfectly what He was sent to do.

2. There's little resemblance of the heavenly to the human parenthood. God created by Himself out of absolute if mysterious love, while people conceive quite often mindlessly, without a shred of love, and never truly by themselves. On the other hand, what human parents would put their child through Christ's suffering even for the universe's sake, especially if they were omnipotent and could save the world some other way? Trying to comprehend the incomprehensible by imaging God's "feelings" or "thoughts" seems naïve, or does it? God became man after all… although His divine nature could not have been affected by the Incarnation. And yet He did (and does) feel and think as we do.

3. The Annunciation did not reveal the full extent of God's plan to Mary (or Joseph). Would she welcome it if she knew the suffering and horror of her son's death? Wouldn't she try to protect Him or at least

share in His misery? What did they actually know, Mary and Joseph? How did Jesus "grow in wisdom"? Are all of the chilling accounts from the apocryphal books completely baseless? What is the truth?

4. Father precedes Son, however eternal both are… God's Word (Holy Spirit?) is His will, applied instantaneously and eternally (retroactively in human terms of space/time). Christ saved/redeemed the ancients as well as transformed our condition (not nature though).

5. Peace may involve some numbness, inactivity, and eventually anxiety of not doing enough. On the other hand, frantic desires to act for the action's sake lead to hasty decisions and premature attempts to accomplish anything, usually at the wrong time. Not to mention forgetting God's role and His ultimate authority over our lives. The greatest mystery: why did God choose "littleness and darkness"?

God becomes hidden in a human child, defying expectations and challenging faith. We are never aware of the full reality and sometimes any reality at all.

1. God has acquired in Jesus' person human consciousness/self-awareness and potential/temptations to sin. At the same time He fused, permeated, or at least intimately exposed human nature to divinity. Human history became irrevocably sacred, and all -- past and future -- generations have now been involved in the eternal act of salvation.

2. The very first example for Christians is Christ's birth: unexpected, inconspicuous, seemingly accidental. It just happened, without anybody's taking a lasting notice, the consequences remaining hidden for thirty years or longer. The extremely, provocatively humble beginnings. Who would have thought? And yet, God became man in most abject conditions, deprived of everything except love -- His God's and His parents'.

3. Christ was entrusted to human parents, subject not only to physical or mental limitations, but also the uncertainty of emotions, doubts, dangers, etc. He was a precocious child but apparently didn't realize -- in His human mind -- His divinity. He was raised in

devotedly Jewish tradition; He originally did not target the whole world (Gentiles) for His message. What if the Jews, including Herod, did accept Him and actually welcome Him as the Messiah? What exactly were Mary and Joseph to do with their (?) child? Wasn't He too much for them? On the other hand, they must have been supported (consciously or not) by the Holy Spirit and given what they needed to raise the divine boy.

4. Couldn't Herod simply have the Wise Men followed to find Jesus' birthplace, if he believed them at all? They must have known the Child's divine nature and were clearly led by God to pay Him homage. On the other hand, why put Jesus and Family in jeopardy by such a high-profile visit? What exactly did everybody feel: awe, uncertainty, fear of unknown, hope? How did Jesus behave as a normal human infant -- sleeping, crying… How "normal" was their life together? Did Joseph love Jesus as his or God's son?

Nothing makes much sense without God's inspiration and help.

1. Jesus is still a Jewish carpenter's son: nothing, except the somewhat unclear adoration by the shepherds and the Magi, indicates His divine nature. Even Simeon's and Anna's prophesies imply only the Hebrew-centered Messiah's role of temporal leadership rather than universal redemption, spiritual elevation and salvation of the whole human race. His parents follow their ancient Hebrew customs, they're unable to realize (will they ever in their lifetimes?) the depth, scope, and absolute immensity of Jesus' life.

2. Joseph proves to be an "unsung hero" of God's story. Mary could do very little without him, actually was entirely dependent -- in earthly terms -- on his good will and faith.

3. God certainly didn't make it easy for His son; the flight and exile into Egypt seem gratuitous as much as Herod's insane bloodthirstiness. How necessary was the innocents' sacrifice? Or is it somewhat related to Jesus' own sacrifice? At any rate, Jesus' childhood seems hardly happy and His family settled.

4. The exile, dangerous journeys, bare necessities of life; how uncertain or downright lost a childhood may appear. The Family could count only on God who directly led them until they settled in Nazareth.

5. Both Mary and Joseph had little, if any, knowledge of Jesus' destiny, and they mustn't have realized His divine nature. Otherwise, how possibly could they not only survive every day face to face with God, but also raise Him in His human form? They must have regarded Mary's son as God's gift, a potential Messiah, but no God by nature.

We are always waiting and dreaming until our time comes.

1. What did Mary and Joseph expect of their son? Joseph taught/trained him to be a carpenter, Mary raised Him to be a devout Jew -- they seem to have not received any instructions from God since their exile. Did they worry about His not marrying, didn't they wait -- despite all the earlier prodigies -- for Him to be a "normal" son? Jesus was certainly waiting, but what really for?

2. Being a human He had His likes and dislikes, fits of anger and bad temper perhaps. Was He always gentle and understanding, with a heavenly detachment from the emotional roller-coaster of life? His thirty hidden years: how much did He Himself realize, or was He simply following God's direct instructions, i.e., was His human mind/body continuously inspired by His divine nature? Did He know every instant what He was expected to do and how? But this would always give Him happiness and serenity, prevent any doubt and most fears, or would it?

3. The first documented "awakening" of Jesus' divine nature and its manifestation…possibly related to His human adolescence? Mary and Joseph's confusion -- again how little they knew, how much had they to be left in the dark. Were they really that happy with their precocious son, didn't they try to place Him more down to earth, didn't they -- forgetting God's messages or doubting their reality (taking them for illusions) -- try to make Jesus an ordinary Jew, raise Him as any Jewish parents would do? There seems to prevail a run-of-the-mill, inauspicious atmosphere around Jesus in those thirty years.

4. Isn't the fight of darkness against light, of death against life, over? Hasn't Christ conquered death and evil, hasn't the Liar lost his war even if he still wins some battles? We do struggle to win our battles but the war is over! So even "evil" people have a chance and are not irretrievably lost.

5. Money certainly cannot buy happiness, nor can power or other earthly successes… It's only the godless who crave for illusory happiness in riches and are envious of neighbors, greedy and bitter. Wealth itself is of course neutral and actually revealed and judged when disposed of. Only fools can claim credit for anything and, on the other hand, blame God for their failures. Christ's kingdom is "not of this earth." He rules by His spiritual superiority, by His divine authority with which no human power can compare. And its essence is love, absolute and unimaginable, which only God can bestow.

6. Lord, you make me cry or laugh, you do what you wish with me. I only beg you to help me overcome my inherent sinfulness; to be at peace more than at war

with myself; to discern, accept, and follow your will; to remember how happy I am.

My faith rather than deeds may save me; I must pray and love.

1. Jesus embarks on His fateful mission, John's baptism being the symbolic (or is it, in light of some apocryphal accounts?) and transitional step to becoming Christ and revealing His divine nature. Did His human mind grasp the immensity of the endeavor? Did His parents talk to Him about the prodigies accompanying His birth? Were they happy and understanding when He left them? Did John consult with Him before his own mission? Were there any comparable religious figures around at that time? Would Jesus need John's assurance that He is actually Christ?

2. A human Jesus (as the divine Christ was beyond his reach) is tempted by Satan, rather crudely, for hunger, pride, and power -- but not for other, more subtle desires such as marriage/family, a peaceful life as a respected scholar and sage… Anyway, Jesus is showing, even before His divine nature's

manifestation, that His humanity can overcome sin or at least not succumb to it again if released of Adam's original fall.

3. Yes, I realize that Christ's is the only way and it is Love, but how to implement my convictions and function effectively in this world? How to overcome my reticence and shyness, not to feel paralyzed by embarrassment and fears of ridicule and inadequacy. How to live my faith without losing and undermining it? How to preserve and defend my dignity while serving and humbling myself before those who are not necessarily my betters? Even Jesus spoke and acted harshly on occasions, rejected people, antagonized potential followers…rather than winning them over or -- even simpler -- confirming their faith. He could do anything with a person, persuade anybody, so why didn't He always?

Follow God's way, not man's. Discern the former by love.

1. John does seem to have launched Jesus on His mission: not only did he have Jesus "confirmed," but also provided two of his own disciples. Nevertheless, the

inspired account of those events is surprisingly sketchy and open to broad interpretations or speculation. John's role wasn't in any way peripheral as he was quite instrumental in the startup of Jesus' public ministry. Would even God need human "sponsorship" in this world, an "introduction" into human society? Or is it all just our images inspired by God's condescending attitude, His desire to help us accept His truth? At any rate, being fully human Jesus may have had infinitely more doubts about His divine mission than we could ever imagine, suffer, or sustain. Who on earth could convince Him about His divinity, and yet He certainly needed that!

2. Christ selected workingmen like himself as disciples, and they promptly abandoned their families and lifestyle to follow an itinerant teacher. They must have seen Christ's light and yet were undistinguished, common folk. Did they ask themselves what they were doing? What did they expect of Jesus? They weren't by nature thinkers, philosophers, revolutionaries; they must have been drawn by Christ's magnetic personality and later by miraculous deeds and prophesies. They were chosen and yet they had to choose themselves by

the virtue of their free will. Nevertheless, they became apostles without much effort on their part, perhaps not very willingly. It's been according to God's, not man's ways.

3. Not my will, but Thine be done. And yet how fearful and attached to this world man continues to feel. Money provides apparent security and small comforts of life, but of course can't buy love and happiness. In the final analysis, it means -- like power -- nothing and becomes relatively important only when being spent, without any undue preoccupation.

4. Christ's divine nature takes over (prompted by Mary?) and Jesus performs His first public miracle, sanctifying marriage and wine. (Nothing wrong with having a good time, no ascetic features apparent in Jesus.) The miracle must have been received with gratitude not only by the host but also his drunken company… Was Jesus Himself intoxicated? After all, it's a human experience. God does have a sense of humor and may enjoy a good laugh. (One of the reasons for our creation.)

5. Overall, Jesus’ selection of His disciples and the place/circumstance of His first miracle are as improbable as His birth. It’s just beyond human comprehension to see God’s point and ways. But whose gift is our reason? Or maybe it’s only supposed to remind us about its limitations.

Forget, abandon the past; live, celebrate, love the present; hope for a better future.

1. Could Jesus’ pronouncement before His townsfolk -- who knew Him only as a local carpenter’s son -- be received as humbly revealing? Christ seems to be struggling against unbelief and prejudice -- and fails. He somehow cannot find the right words and tone, seems helpless and lost among His own neighbors. Isn’t His humanity too distressingly human, faltering, and pitiful? Or could His attempt to show off have been rejected by the Father?

2. My desires/thoughts come from God or Satan or simply myself (neutral). My response/deeds should vary depending on my perceived source of the inspiration. Only in the neutral case, it doesn’t really matter.

3. Christ did take care of both bodies and souls; the former aren't thus insignificant, or His mercy wouldn't be directed to alleviate physical suffering. The Beatitudes -- how to be happy: open, innocent, and humble heart ("poor" spirit); acceptance of suffering and sad reversals of fortune ("mourning"); unflinching desire to serve and live for God; mercy and forgiveness; inner and outer peace, reconciliation; courage to do and pronounce God's will in spite of opposition and all physical and emotional dangers (embarrassments, ridicule).

4. One pleases God by denying oneself, i.e., ignoring or sacrificing one's ambitions and personal gratification for God's sake (but not necessarily others'). In this country of plenty, are there any "deserving" poor? Should we reinforce sinful behaviors by supporting those "poor" who violate God's commands? Incidentally, very few of the "deserving" poor are unhappy or want any material help. On the other hand, can we pass judgments on others' sins? Can we question God's mercy or usurp His powers? Aren't we supposed to serve and love sinners, which we are ourselves?

5. Follow your conscience not only to refrain from sin but also when trying to do good. Think and speak the truth, do not deceive yourself and others either by wishful thinking or horrific imaginings. Above all: LOVE AND YOU'LL NEVER GO WRONG.

Please, Lord, show me your Truth and help me see, hear, and speak.

1. We see only momentarily, get glimpses of Truth, rejoice at inspired insights, feel God's love, sense His wisdom, believe unhesitatingly -- and then go blind again, fear or ignore life, hate ourselves and others, and let the Devil do with us what he pleases.

2. It is not enough to contemplate, to rejoice at God's favors and love; it's imperative to proclaim, share and spread out the Good News, to inspire or educate others. How to overcome, though, the fears, reticence, etc. Should one force oneself to start one's "public ministry" and be God's ineffective witness in an unreceptive crowd?

3. I realize I fall short of Jesus' ideal, but perhaps my time is yet to come, and I simply need to wait, pray, and listen. I still may need Christ's visit to my home, God's more clear instructions what to do… Even if something looks good but generates, or is accompanied by, fear and anxiety, or results in desolation, it shouldn't probably be pursued. Good and noble impulses may or may not make sense to God and produce lasting happiness or contentment.

The willing spirit may overcome and control the weak body -- with a prayer.

1. Feed the hungry, give sight to the blind, comfort the suffering… Act, not only talk, however beautifully, or contemplate/meditate, however deeply. Help people in their mundane needs, keep to the earth as others, yourself included, are still on it. Do not despise or neglect (but don't grow attached to either) the world and its reality.

2. Peter, by God's inspiration, recognized Christ as the Messiah, which did not, however, prevent him from denying his God all the same not long afterward, or

arguing about earthly honors. When will this human folly end? How can I change my own nature?

3. Jesus is tempted by His own disciples to abandon His mission and rebukes the same Peter who recognized Him as Christ not long ago. The agony seems to be commencing now, long before the actual arrest and death, since Jesus has already realized all the details of His fate, and even the glorious resurrection appears somewhat more distant than the terrifying human experience that precedes it.

We mean nothing and can do as much without faith and love.

1. Little faith, large fears, never-ending doubts -- was Jesus really surprised by His apostles' human weaknesses? More was revealed to these men than to anybody else, yet they couldn't help it and hardly changed, retaining their mentality of most ordinary folk.

2. It isn't the paraplegic's friends' devotion as much as the local leaders' short-lived memory that is puzzling. It is perfectly conceivable that people

would try to have their family members or friends healed at any cost. It's more difficult to comprehend how soon people forget miracles and take their blessings for granted. Even worse, they may grow to hate the very person they used to love and admire if the reversal suits their interests or just conforms to a majority's view.

3. Again, little faith and doubts/fears almost sink Peter… On the other hand, only Jesus was fully aware of His mission and power, following the Father's blueprints rather than His own desires and plans. Incidentally, would the latter have been any different?

Was Jesus' humanity perfect? (Adam's before the original sin) Can ours be? Is it not dependent on God? And yet, we -- as Christ eventually did -- may become perfect in following God's will.

1. Jesus' plan seems to be to spread the Good News among His fellow Jews only, as He sends out his apostles and declares Samaria and the Gentiles' territory off-

limits. Incidentally, this might be the first test for the apostles to become preachers and missionaries.

2. His not very charitable expulsion of the Temple merchants signifies Jesus' human anger/temper. His antagonistic attitude toward Jewish authorities doesn't make it easier for anybody. In light of so many prophets before Him, couldn't Jesus show more understanding and patience with the suspicious rulers who, after all, tried to follow God's commands and not undermine His Mosaic laws?

3. Yet another confrontation as if this "non-emergency" healing couldn't wait (even now elective surgeries are not done on Sundays). Why doesn't Jesus show more love and understanding to His fellow Jews, still brothers in faith? Unless God has already decided to separate or even exclude them from the New Covenant.

God's terms aren't man's, and man can only pray to learn the former.

1. Lazarus' resurrection (followed by others) shows Christ's power over death and anticipates His own

rising from the dead, albeit in a transformed state. Again though, Martha's faith seemed critical in Jesus' performing the miracle. Can the latter occur without the former?

2. Why was Jesus surprised by a Gentile's faith? Did his human (Jewish) nature refuse to recognize the universal need and yearning for absolute or at least supernatural (healing) powers? How amazingly human Jesus' mentality appears in spite of His divine actions -- as if the Man part of God was but a tool, unaware of the Master's designs or even deeper truths.

3. Did the transfiguration occur for the sake of Jesus' companions rather than Christ himself? No witness to it should any longer have had doubts of Jesus' nature. Incidentally, what possibly could He have talked about with Moses and Elijah, respectively the author and the most prominent prophet of the Old Covenant? Jesus' "progress" in anticipation of the transition to the New Covenant?

4. Sinless, Christ did not make any mistakes, even though He could have on account of His free will and human

nature. Yet His actions were mistakes in human (Jewish) terms: undermining the Law, authorities, accepted norms…

I still know nothing, but let God decide and inspire me to do what must be right.

1. How much can/should we share without jeopardizing our own functioning in this world? In a welfare state, our taxes are supposed to support/subsidize the poor. Wouldn't commitments of time, talents, and above all love be more important? One can't buy true (disinterested) love, and also one can't live without it.

2. Jesus knew how illusory and transient the people's admiration and devotion were, and yet He accepted them, as any human would if only for temporary consolation. Or was this a resigned following of the Father's script to provoke the Jewish authorities and precipitate/seal His fate?

3. The last days of Jesus' human presence on earth, His last human joys and sorrows. His desire/need of comfort and

simple pleasures to perhaps blunt the pangs of grief and terror at the upcoming agony and death.

WEEK 4. THE NEW COVENANT ESTABLISHED AND SEALED, BUT HOW DO I RELATE?

1. Jesus chooses the Jewish Passover for His establishing the New Covenant and offering His own sacrifice that will not be passed over. Why would the destruction and death strike Jesus rather than His (God's) enemies this time? Why would the latter be still preserved for the coming millennia? Out of the old sentiments and the unbreakable Old Covenant?

2. Jesus didn't "disguise" his divinity because he was human after all, and his human nature was no different from ours. It's possible, however mysterious, that he wasn't aware -- in his human heart and mind -- of his divinity until his very death.

3. The Old Covenant was sealed with animal blood sacrificed by the Jews. The New Covenant involved Jesus' human blood sacrificed by God, with the Jews as executioners. Could it be, however, that the Jews had

the opportunity to accept Jesus and just renew their covenant -- as suggested by prophets -- and again limit its application to themselves? Jesus didn't seem to have cared much about the Gentiles after all…

4. Complete submission, humility, a serving attitude precede the agony, death, but also the glorious resurrection. However, what to do if love simply isn't there? If frustration, helplessness, suspicions, or just laziness take over? How to keep up one's enthusiasm, faith, devotion, trust? Again, only prayer and God's help will do.

5. It's amazing that Christ, being aware of His mission and God's will, suffered so much anguish and pain, more so than some of His saints, unless His condition was made to resemble that of an ordinary man, or was part of God's redemptive plan for humanity.

I can't follow Jesus to destruction without a clear command from God.

1. I may have difficulties relating to Jesus' agony because I'm relatively safe and at peace, as actually

most people in the Western (Christian) world are. On the other hand, the past experiences -- saturated with suffering but quite inspiring -- put me much closer to Christ. Can't I assume that, my spiritual ordeals/torments being temporarily over, it's time to accept God's will with peace? Or is it rather the Devil's anesthetics to prevent me from following God's incarnation on earth, sharing His feelings and plight, accepting and appreciating the Redemption?

2. The Last Night is unfolding, early spring, cold. Jesus regains His composure, confounds some of his enemies but his defiance seals his fate anyhow. Did He have any chance in this confrontation? Did he count on one? I'm writing nonsense, I can't penetrate the Mystery, I can't truly feel anything.

God the Father chooses people and time, nothing ever occurs without His saving knowledge. He fixes whatever we screw up.

1. The figure of the Silent Christ. Silence is more telling than human words. God's Word is not man's. How could Christ possibly explain to Pilate what it's all

about? He did nevertheless, to some extent, without speaking.

2. Again, a mental/emotional block prevents my following Jesus. Distractions multiply; prayer brings peace but no inspiration or even deeper sympathy with Christ. All seems so distant and my efforts to live and feel futile.

3. The events assume the air of inevitability, set in motion or condoned by God. The crowd having sung Hosanna on Sunday, clamors for crucifixion on Friday. The all-powerful Roman governor is reduced to a mob-pleaser. Christ is reconciled with His mission's end on the earth and hardly defends Himself. Was this exactly what God had envisioned?

4. As Jesus pointed out, the authorities (Pilate) could only do what God let them, they were never more than clumsy, inconvenient tools in His hand.

Never cease to trust God -- even, or especially when silent, hidden, and doubtful. We are born for Him and die in Him. We love and are consoled by Him, but He sets the right time for everything.

1. God-Man is abandoned by His disciples, friends, family, admirers…goes through extreme suffering; no man will ever accuse Him of not feeling what we experience…

2. Christ continues His unabated suffering, is mercilessly and unceremoniously pinned to the wood in the routine manner of, and between, common criminals. And yet the execution has a chilling air of fulfillment, of Jesus' closing, in complete submission and passivity, His mission on earth.

3. Despite efforts my involvement remains skin-deep, with most silly distractions taking over my mind and even heart. I wish I were more inspired, a better man in general, less selfish, more loving, with greater faith. And I certainly wish I were happier and more appreciative of God's wonders and the beauty that surrounds me; that I would never forget Christ's redeeming sacrifice, that I could find peace and

consolation even in suffering and accept my life as it is with gratitude.

4. In His last minutes on earth Jesus reaches the bottom of human misery, loneliness, and abandonment. No consolation; possibly dark despair punctuated with passersby's jeers; apparently hopeless and senseless agony. And yet, could God's silence be more promising? Jesus had to be fully human -- without any divine premonitions -- to offer a credible example, especially in His agony.

When it's finished, it starts anew. To conquer death one needs to die.

1. Jesus' death, in charity, is as exemplary as His life, again in humanity rather than divinity: It is Man who is born, suffers, and dies; it is God who performs miracles, teaches, forgives sins, and establishes the New Covenant. We, of course, must look up to the man, imitate and follow Him whatever it takes. Be truthful in death as much as in life, because how we die determines how we shall live. Having been conceived in God's eternal mind, our souls -- in His image and

likeness -- are incarnated, pass through life on earth, and return to their Creator. The passage, including the final event -- separation or liberation from the time/space constraints -- sets our individual unique essence in relation to, and as a somewhat enriched part of, God's Kingdom. Beyond the earthly space and time, even our bodies may survive having undergone Christ-like glorification, since their physical decomposition does not apply to, has no effect on their transformed state (resurrection) in eternity.

2. Christ dies, faithful to the end, a death most despicable and ignominious in human terms and most glorious and redeeming in God's. No one can outdo Him in suffering and glory, yet I can try to imitate Him by humbly serving others, giving them my unconditional love and respect. This is what people need most -- always and everywhere. However, I must do everything for God's glory rather than mine, for others' sake rather than to feed my ego. The image and real presence of the Cross should certainly help here. Expect nothing in return -- no reward, no adulation, no gratitude, no human love…

3. The mysterious transformation, Jesus' glorification, begins or rather is effected by God's Word that infuses eternity into man's world. Christ is united with the Father, reconciles the human race with the Creator, and elevates its condition, if not nature, to the divine level.

Love: transcend my ego, feel for and share with fellow human beings -- they at least as important as I am -- expecting nothing in return. Pray for all of us as we all need God's grace.

1. I can't feel "a simple and graceful union" with Jesus the man because of the differences in background and social setting, not to mention religion (the Jewish Law). The union forms by sharing the same human condition, suffering, faith/hope in God's love and eternal life.

2. Clearly nobody expected Christ to rise from the dead, even though the Jewish authorities suspected His disciples of attempting "tricks." Jesus' story seemed to be over -- one more impostor or prophet is removed

and life goes on. Actually, the High Priest overestimated the disciples who were in fact scared to death, bewildered and disorganized. Christ's mission failed as no one believed in him any more.

3. A strong sense of God's absolute presence and creative/inspiring powers -- I exist only because of, and for, Him. His incarnation designed to elevate human condition, if not nature, including humility and suffering. Continuing redemption of man's sins; incessant, unfaltering companionship, friendship, and love. Self-abandonment -- Thy will be done, even or especially when it involves sacrifices. Which is painful, unappetizing, sorrowful, depressing, even though it leads to happiness in the long run.

WEEK 5. DEATH IS NO MORE, NOR OBLIVION NOR DESPAIR, PROVIDED ONE BELIEVES.

1. Absolute joy and happiness, a complete reversal of the earthly misery, a taste of eternal life and glory. The anguish, doubts, mortal fear fade away and an exulted peace fills Mary's heart. Nothing, she hopes, can undermine her Son's mission and separate Him from her.

She is, in fact, God's mother and will remain so irrevocably in the human history,

2. God has written Moses' tablets; Christ wrote nothing, even after His resurrection. Why did He rely on the spoken word for the New Covenant? Would the Holy Spirit and its everlasting presence more than compensate for the lack of etched stone that might disappear anyhow? Or does the deed speak more eloquently than any words?

3. The first person to see the risen Christ was Mary Magdalene rather than His mother, and she may have been more scared than happy. Man seems unable to accept God's signs without His (Holy Spirit's) strong help as the divine simply goes beyond human comprehension and initially terrifies rather than exalts.

4. Peter is still confused and hesitating to believe… If the apostles, the very chosen ones, couldn't easily believe, how can we? Well, we can't unless the Holy Spirit graciously helps us.

Lord’s consolation and peace -- pray for and receive.

1. Not accidentally, the first gift of the Lord to His apostles was peace, then the Holy Spirit to make them act with Jesus’ authority. They needed first to calm down, comprehend, believe; then they needed the confidence and abilities to act as God’s representatives on earth. Before His appearance they were but a bunch of frightened, clueless people.

2. It’s one thing to know and another to feel and believe with one’s whole heart, beyond all doubts and weariness. Love and faith must be felt permeating and burning one’s heart and leaving, generating the only true and lasting happiness/peace. But this cannot be decreed, prescribed, or self-induced, although it must be accepted and welcomed when God’s grace stirs one’s soul and lets the Holy Spirit fill it with divine essence.

3. Despite Christ’s victory over death and evil, we fear and are exposed to them as much as ever. And rather than looking forward to God’s glory, we cling to this miserable world and continue to suffer physically and

mentally, understanding nothing, and more often than not making no sense of our lives at all.

Forgetfulness, concupiscence -- be on guard.

1. How repulsive my soul may appear to God as even I feel (sometimes) how rotten it is. Like Thomas, I continue to doubt or ignore the Lord's presence and I persevere in self-deception, complacency, arrogance, and foolish pride.

2. Christ's appearance didn't change much in the first week after the Resurrection: the Apostles were still waiting (for instructions?) or doubting, no revolution seemed to be forthcoming, business went on as usual… The Redemption passed virtually unnoticed.

3. In case we abuse or misuse our freedom, can't we pray to God to take it away from us? Can't we voluntarily forfeit our lousy free will so that we could only do good, praise the Lord in peace, enjoying a happy union with Him, reminiscent of Eden? On the other hand, we can't change God's image in us, i.e., divest of any of its features.

4. Christ is not easily recognizable even by His own disciples… He is more hidden and mysterious as His state has changed at the Resurrection, and He appears only to those who want to believe, who are prepared to accept Him, who have -- or at least are open to -- faith.

God's kingdom and glory IS with us, here and now, till the end of time.

1. What would Christ have to do to make their disciples realize, feel the meaning of His resurrection; to make them act and believe; to convince them that they are the future of mankind and the universe, which their actions would transform into a new world, a new civilization unparalleled in human history? Is even God's (self-limiting) will helpless in confrontation with human stubbornness and idiocy? But how had man acquired this lousy nature? Why was he (Adam) so dim-witted as to risk his Creator's anger and condemnation? Why do we succumb so easily to temptations and end up taking the same risks? Who are we? Who is Jesus before and after the Resurrection?

How does His human condition differ from ours? Why can't we truly share it now? We still fear, doubt, sin…

2. Why can't we always appreciate the obvious glory and love of the Lord? Why do we hold God responsible for our shortcomings and sins? We are His creatures and are redeemed, reaccepted, and represented in Heaven by Christ at that. Why can't we enjoy this status to its fullest? Why can't we always love as we want, Godlike? Why do we continue to struggle, to feel miserable, incomplete, uncertain, fearful, lost? Why is our new condition -- children of God -- not more apparent? Well, because we choose to close our eyes and ears, to forget the basics of our faith, and to replace God by our idolatrous worldly goals that we pursue unrelentingly, offering them sacrifices due only to God.

3. Despite so many appearances of Christ, the Jewish authorities remained unimpressed… What's wrong with them? Why couldn't they accept God's change, however incomprehensible, in handling humans, the total revelation expressed by the Incarnation and testing

man's fate/condition to redeem it and to make it sensible again?

Elect the loving submission to God, remember Christ's redemptive Cross and Resurrection, pray for and accept the Holy Spirit. Live without guilt.

1. The Apostles did not get it as they continued to expect Israel's glory… They were unable to transcend their narrow Jewishness and realize that God may be willing to extend His interest to other peoples, especially since the Jews again have rejected Him.

2. Despite His physical absence He is with us, and nothing, nobody can separate us from Him. But His presence is conditional on our faith; He can do nothing unless we -- exercising our free will -- accept Him. Only we can separate Him from us.

3. Again, the Apostles continued to pray in the Temple and missed Christ's message to proclaim and spread the New Covenant.

4. If one is supposed to fix one's eye on heaven and forget earth, how can one effectively act on earth? Unless one is simply to practice and implement the heavenly rules on earth knowing that Christ has already transformed human condition and made this possible. We can always invoke Christ's example and live in His glory, doing what must be done without any earthly considerations.

5. How permanent were the "tongues of fire," how long did the Apostles feel their effect? Or did the Holy Spirit appear/inspire them whenever they prayed and believed? How did the Apostles expect to change/overcome human nature and reach sainthood? By the nonhuman/supernatural will… and again prayer/faith/love.

6. One can't proclaim the Good News without the Holy Spirit's inspiration, and even then the task isn't necessarily joyful or rewarding; more often than not one faces ridicule and contempt, suspicion and hostility. On the other hand, sincere faith and inspired words, calm and gentle demeanor, quiet internal strength may convince -- sooner or later --

the most hardened cynic. The key is uninterested, unconditional, God-like love, and matching deeds. One must never give up, one has to persevere as long as one lives -- with God and only God calling it quits (or rather it finished/fulfilled).

7. Love means a persistent dedication, self-abandonment/denial for the beloved. New dimensions open up in the lover's eyes, as God reveals more of His nature. It's unearthly joy and lasting happiness. It's the urge to share, give, help. But also it's a time of emotions running high, often uncontrollably; a time of unpredictable behavior and sadness/vulnerability; a time of tears, painful misunderstandings, intense imagining, self-deceit and confusion replacing reality by wishful thinking.

8. Everybody does have a place in God's plan, a destiny to fulfill -- although in a range allowing for free will and modification by one's prayer to God who can and does change anything He wishes. ("Nothing is impossible with God.") Well, He, not us. Since it wasn't possible to take away Jesus' cup, we can't really complain about ours. We must accept, and be

grateful for, His will because we are His creatures, and any form of existence -- arguably including suffering -- is infinitely better than nothingness.

9. Thank you for all Thy gifts, and especially the capacity for love; for the security of your irrevocable love; for our immortal and ever-young soul; for being.

10. We don't even know what we should want and pray for, i.e., we're completely helpless and clueless without the Holy Spirit's inspiration. The more we turn off our egos and ignore banal earthly desires, the more we let the Spirit guide us and are truly happy in the long run. The alternative is a painful, fruitless, and never-ending struggle with oneself permeated by anxiety, unquenchable thirst, bitterness, and despair… We just can't help it, that's our heritage as children of God; our choice will always remain a loving submission or a hopeless rebellion. There's no third way.

www.ingramcontent.com/pod-product-compliance
Ingram Content Group UK Ltd.
Pitfield, Milton Keynes, MK11 3LW, UK
UKHW051135260726
13967UKWH00010B/3063